TEACH YOURSELF TO PLAY THE FOLK HARP

30th Anniversary Edition

First Book in a Series by SYLVIA WOODS

All Pieces Arranged by Sylvia Woods

DEDICATION

This book is dedicated to everyone who uses it to learn to play the harp, and to those whose lives will be enriched and enlivened by their music.

THANKS TO:

Katharine, Shawna, and Heidi for being great guinea pigs . . .
Chris and Teresa for their contributions . . .
Janet, Dwight, and Dinah for their photos . . .
Robin for his knowledge and suggestions . . .
Conway and Marjorie for their special assistance . . .
Don for his time and expertise . . .
Lou Anne for her encouragement . . .
and Tommy for his patience, help, and love.

THE "TYPESETTING" OF THIS BOOK

I created this book long before the advent of home computers, desktop publishing, or music software. In those days, if you wanted a fancy typeface for a flier, you could buy transparent sheets of dry transferable letters in your chosen font and size and then rub off the letters you needed, one by one, onto a sheet of paper. This was a tedious and laborious task, and if you made a mistake it was hard to correct. Artwork, symbols, and musical notes were also available in this format.

Now, here's an amazing little-known fact. Every note in this book was rubbed off in this manner, one at a time, from a transfer sheet! Here's how I did this arduous task. I started with a sheet of music staff paper, with the 5-line staves. I rubbed off the appropriate clefs for each line, and the time signature. Then, one by one, I rubbed off the notes with the correct time value. I rubbed off the fingerings from another transfer sheet in the same way. Then, using a pen and a ruler, I drew in the bar lines, beams, brackets, ties, endings, and other symbols.

I typed the small text throughout the book on an IBM Selectric typewriter. The larger text in the titles and chapter headings was rubbed off, one letter at a time, from a transfer sheet.

Photos by Janet Williamson, Dwight Caswell, Sylvia Woods, and Tom Woods
Illustrations on pages 77 and 78 by Cristina McAllister

Sylvia Woods Harp Center
Woods Music & Books
PO Box 223434, Princeville HI 96722

www.harpcenter.com

ISBN 978-0-936661-42-1

CONTENTS

INTRODUCTION
FROM THE EARLIER EDITIONS

Many people feel drawn to the magical and spiritual qualities of the harp, which has come to us through the mists of time. In my travels around the world playing the Celtic harp, I have observed an exciting resurgence of interest in folk harps. A growing number of craftsmen are making harps, and more and more people are learning to play them. Everywhere I have performed, people have approached me asking for information on where to obtain harps and how to play them. I enjoy being able to help people realize their dreams of becoming harpers; that is why I have written this book.

You don't need a teacher or any previous musical training to learn to play the harp (although either of these will be helpful). This book will teach you what you need to know. Each lesson is a bit more advanced than the previous one. Every once in a while the pieces will seem to be a lot harder than the ones before. Try not to let this discourage you. Look on the more difficult pieces as challenges that will help expand your abilities. Pieces like *Scarborough Fair, Trip to Sligo*, and *Shenandoah* are not easy to master; but once you do, you will have accomplished a great deal!

This book teaches you the basics of folk harp playing. Once you've completed this book you have a wide selection of music to try. For example, I have written books of Christmas music, Irish music, church music, wedding music, popular music, and more, all arranged for the folk harp. Write to the address below and we'll send you a free catalog.

Please write to me and let me know how you are doing. I love to hear from harpers who are using this book, so I can give any assistance. Also, if you would like help in finding a good harp, 1 can refer you to several excellent harpmakers who make fine, high-quality instruments.

My harp brings me so much pleasure and a feeling of freedom. I'm sure your harp will do the same for you, and you and your harp will do that for others. With your harp and this book you are off on a great adventure. Enjoy it!

Sylvia Woods

Sylvia Woods
Woods Music & Books, Inc.
Sylvia Woods Harp Center
P.O. Box 816
Montrose, CA 91021 USA
www.harpcenter.com

A CD of Sylvia Woods playing the pieces in this book is available. Sylvia has also created a DVD giving detailed instructions and helpful hints, as well as showing you how to play the pieces in this book. These products are available from the store where you purchased this book, or from the Sylvia Woods Harp Center at the address and website above.

INTRODUCTION
TO THE 30TH ANNIVERSARY EDITION

30 years ago, in 1978, when I wrote this book, the harp world was a far different place than it is today. There were only a handful of craftspeople making harps, and they often had waiting lists of a year or more. Because of this, harps were not as easy to purchase as they are today. There were also only a few recordings (LPs) of music performed on lever or folk harps.

When I began teaching, I realized that there was also a lack of music for the folk harp. Most of the music available was for the pedal harp, or for young children whose legs weren't long enough to reach the pedals. I couldn't find books that were suitable for the people who were becoming interested in the resurgence of the folk harp. That is why I wrote this book.

Folk harp teachers were also hard to find at that time. There were lots of pedal harp teachers, but a vast majority of them were not interested in teaching anything that didn't have pedals. This is why I entitled the book "Teach Yourself," because in those days, that was the only option for most players. And thousands of players have done just that . . . they have taught themselves to play just using this book, and also perhaps the video or the DVD.

Luckily, today you don't have to do it on your own. There are thousands of teachers throughout the US (and other parts of the world!) who are ready and willing to help you learn to play the harp. I highly recommend that you start lessons with a teacher as soon as possible. No matter how good a "teach yourself" book may be, the guidance and feedback you get from a teacher is invaluable. It is easy to get into bad habits without someone "looking over your shoulder" and showing you the correct way. Bad habits are harder to fix later than if you learn correctly from the beginning.

The "Thanks To" section on page 2 of this book is from the original edition. On the first line you'll see that I thank "Katharine, Shawna, and Heidi for being great guinea pigs." These were three of my first students, and were the first people to learn the harp by using this book. I'd like to give you an update on them. Katharine has been "taking some time off" from the harp, but has recently begun to play again on both lever and pedal harp. Shawna was 11 years old when she started lessons with me. She's now a professional harp player named Shawna Selline, and we sell her CDs on our website. And Heidi is Heidi Spiegel, a harpist who has been working for me since 1988 and who is an invaluable asset to the Sylvia Woods Harp Center. She is also a fine artist who has illustrated the covers of over a dozen of my books and pieces of sheet music.

In this 30th Anniversary Edition, I have kept all of the music pages exactly as they were in the first edition. Only the introduction and appendix pages have been revised.

There are no sharps or flats in any of the pieces in this book. At the time I wrote this book, sharping levers were not nearly as good, or as accurate, as they are today. They generally did not give an accurate pitch when engaged, and often wore away the strings. Many harps sold at that time didn't have any levers at all. That's why you don't need any sharping levers to play the pieces in this book. (See pages 73 and 74 for more information on how to use sharping levers.)

HOW TO USE THIS BOOK

The range of notes used in this book goes from the G that is 10 strings below middle C, up
to the C that is 2 octaves above middle C. If you have a small harp that doesn't have some
of the low strings, you have several choices when playing pieces that have notes lower than
your harp. On many of the pieces, you can play all the notes with both hands an octave
higher than written, and this will keep the music in the range for your harp. Or, if there are
only a few notes that your harp is missing, you can just play those individual notes an
octave higher, keeping the rest of the notes in the range as written in the music.

You do not need any sharping levers on your harp to play the music in this book because there are no
sharps or flats in any of the pieces. See pages 73 and 74 for more information on sharps, flats, and the
use of sharping levers in other harp music.

I highly recommend that you take lessons from a qualified harp teacher while you are learning to play
the harp. Although you can "teach yourself," the feedback and guidance from a teacher will make you a
much better harp player and give you greater enjoyment and success.

This book is designed to be studied consecutively from beginning to end. Each chapter introduces a new
technique or concept. Don't be tempted to skip around. Be sure you understand the material and can
play the pieces in each lesson before going on.

I have created two companion products that you'll find useful while learning from this book. On the
companion CD I play all of the pieces in the book, so you can hear how the music is supposed to sound.
The informative companion DVD is extremely helpful, particularly if you are teaching yourself without
the aid of a teacher. I give more detailed instruction about the concepts and techniques presented in the
book, and point out places in the music where you need to pay particular attention. You can also see
my hand position and playing technique as you watch me play all of the pieces. You should be able to
purchase either of these companion products from the store where you purchased this book. Or, you
can order them directly from me at www.harpcenter.com.

If you'd like a copy of the lyrics for the songs in this book, they are available for purchase in a booklet
that also contains the lyrics from my Hymns and Wedding Music for All Harps book. However, you
may also download the lyrics for free at www.harpcenter.com/lyrics.

A SPECIAL NOTE FOR PIANISTS AND OTHER MUSICIANS

Having taught hundreds of people how to play the harp, I have observed that beginners who are already
accomplished musicians, particularly pianists, tend to try to progress too fast, without taking the time to
create a good foundation of basic technique. You may be able to sight-read the music in this book
immediately. However, if you do this, you're probably not playing it correctly with proper hand position
and placing. I can't emphasize enough how vital it is for you to spend time with the first few lessons
playing the pieces very slowly, conscientiously following the placing brackets, watching to be sure your
hand position is correct and your fingers are moving all the way into your palm. Taking the time to stop
and place your fingers in the brackets, even if that means that there are pauses in the music, is much
more important at the beginning than playing the piece in the correct time. Don't be in a hurry. The time
you spend to be sure your basics are solid at the beginning will pay off for years to come.

TYPES AND PARTS OF HARPS

FOLK HARPS or LEVER HARPS

Folk harps can also be called **lever harps, Celtic harps, Irish harps,** or **non-pedal harps**. They range in size from small 20 string lap harps to larger floor harps with up to 40 strings. No matter what name your harp goes by, you can use this book to learn to play your harp.

South American or **Mexican-style harps** are usually played with a slightly different technique than what is presented in this book, and often the string colors are different. However, if you have that type of harp, you can still use this book to learn to play.

Wire-strung or **metal-strung harps** also have their own special playing technique. If you have one of these harps, I suggest that you supplement this book with an additional method book specifically designed for that type of harp.

PEDAL HARPS

Pedal harps are the harps that are played in an orchestra. They are also called **concert harps, orchestral harps,** or **grand harps.** They have between 40 and 47 strings. There are seven pedals which are moved by the harpist's feet, one pedal for each of the seven notes in the scale. The pedals move discs on the neck of the harp which shorten or lengthen the sounding length of the strings, providing sharps, naturals, and flats. Although the title of this book mentions a "Folk Harp," you can also use it to learn to play a pedal harp.

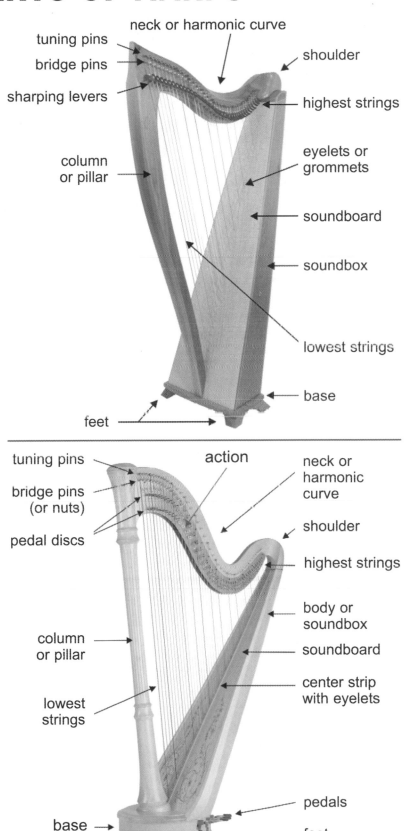

neck or harmonic curve
tuning pins
bridge pins
shoulder
sharping levers
highest strings
column or pillar
eyelets or grommets
soundboard
soundbox
lowest strings
base
feet

tuning pins
action
neck or harmonic curve
bridge pins (or nuts)
shoulder
pedal discs
highest strings
body or soundbox
column or pillar
soundboard
lowest strings
center strip with eyelets
base
pedals
feet

BRIEF HISTORY OF THE FOLK HARP

by Christopher Caswell and Robin Williamson

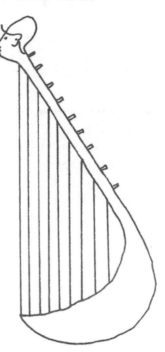

Now that you're learning to play the folk harp, you are carrying on an ancient tradition which has continued for thousands of years. Any culture that had a hunting bow had the fundamental form of a harp, making the harp one of the oldest stringed instruments. These bow harps originated in many areas of the world, and some are still in use today. Carvings, plaques and wall paintings of these harps dating from as early as 3000 B.C. still exist in Egypt and Mesopotamia. Bow harps, such as the one shown on the right, do not have a front pillar (see page 7); rather, they are held together by the tension of the strings, themselves.

The first main improvement of the harp was the addition of a rigid pillar, making a triangular frame harp similar to those of today. This harp was probably much easier to tune than the bow harp, and allowed more choice of scales. There is a small statue from the Cyclades (islands near Greece) dated between 3000 and 2000 B.C. which shows a seated man playing what appears to be a frame harp.

In Ireland, the earliest mention of the harp is about 541 B.C., where the harp was made of willow, and the harper's name was Craftiné. The earliest known depiction of a frame harp in the British Isles is on an 8th Century stone cross in Scotland. Here, as well as in other Celtic countries, harpers were very important and well-respected. They were often poets as well as musicians, and were credited with magical powers. Harpers were required to be able to evoke three different emotions in their audience by their music: Geantraighe, or laughter; Goltraighe, or tears; and Suantraighe, or sleep.

The Ancient Celtic harps used in Ireland and Scotland were strung with combinations of brass and steel wire, and possibly gold and silver. The soundboxes were carved from a single piece of wood. In early Wales, they apparently strung some harps with horsehair, producing a buzzing sound. Later, they too used brass-strung harps.

Gradually, with the coming of Christianity, the invasions of the Vikings, and social disruption and feuding in the British Isles, the harpers lost much of their influence and power, becoming court minstrels and street musicians.

In the 10th Century, Brian Boru, the Irish hero and warrior king, did much to revive the harp in Ireland, founding the Bardic Order which created a musical heritage and tradition which survived 500 years.

About the time of Brian Boru, Irish harpers were traveling to the highlands of Scotland to study in the harping schools there. By the middle ages, however, the trend had reversed and Scots harpers were commonly traveling to Ireland to learn their craft.

One of the three oldest harps from the British Isles is commonly associated with Brian Boru, although its true history is not known. Shown here on the right, it is a low-headed lap harp with 30 strings, and is now housed at Trinity College, Dublin. The other two harps are Scottish; the Queen Mary Harp is almost identical to the Trinity College Harp, and the Lamont Harp is slightly larger.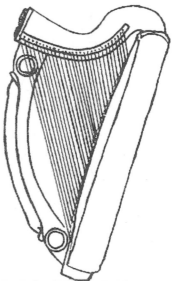

The harp was originally the national instrument of Scotland. Each clan had its own harper who held a position of high esteem. Over centuries of internal feuding among various chieftains, however, the harp was gradually replaced by the more war-like bagpipes. The harp was in full decline in Scotland by the 17th Century.

During the reign of Elizabeth I, the Catholic landowners in Ireland were displaced by Protestant ones. At the same time, the harpers, most of whom were Catholic, fell into disfavor with the government because they supposedly incited rebellion with their songs and music. Once again, the harpers lost status, and many of them fled to Scotland or the continent.

The harps in Europe were gut-strung and generally had narrower, shallower sound-boxes built from several pieces of wood. Here, the harp was often used by troubadours as accompaniment for songs in the new fashion of courtly love and chivalry. Traveling Irish harpers met with great response, their louder instruments making a mark which would lead to the development of the pedal harp in about a century.

The Italians produced a triple-strung harp (with three rows of strings) which the Welsh adopted as their national instrument. The Spanish enjoyed double-strung harps, as well as the single-strung harps which they carried with them to the new world.

Towards the end of the 18th Century, the use of the metal-strung, or Ancient Celtic harp, had died down in Ireland. At a harper's convention in Belfast in 1792, only one player, Denis Hempson, still played in the earlier style with fingernails upon metal strings. The so-called Neo-Celtic harp, which had gut strings, had become more prevalent.

In the early 20th Century, the Celtic revivals in Ireland and Scotland brought new strength to folk harping there, and Neo-Celtic harps were being made in increasing numbers. Beginning in the 1960s, harping has become even more popular in the British Isles and America, and harp building has continued to increase steadily to meet the demand. With more instruments and music books available, use of the folk harp has grown greatly in every field of music.

With your harp, you are contributing to the culture of the future, whose echoes will be heard for centuries to come.

HOLDING THE HARP

It is important to sit properly when playing the harp. Sit in an armless chair or harp bench, with your feet flat on the floor. Don't lean against the back of the chair. Sit behind the soundbox with the harp between your knees and angled a bit towards your right shoulder. Lean the top of the harp towards you until the soundbox rests lightly against your right shoulder. The front of the base of the harp will lift up from the floor. Don't place the harp too close to your neck. You should have enough room to comfortably turn you head to look at the upper strings. When the harp is tilted back properly, the strings should be approximately vertical, and the harp should be lightly balanced against your

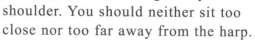

shoulder. You should neither sit too close nor too far away from the harp. Experiment with different stool heights and how close you are sitting to the harp until you find a comfortable position.

If your harp is not tall enough to reach your shoulder, sit on a lower bench, or raise the harp by placing it on a small stool or table, as shown on the left.

SMALL HARPS

To play a lap harp, put it on your lap and lean it back so that the top of the soundbox rests lightly against your right shoulder, as shown in the photo on the right. Experiment with the angle of the harp by moving the base closer to your knees, or closer to your body, until you find a position that feels comfortable and secure.

Many people find it easier to play a lap harp by setting it on a chair or stool in front of them, instead of balancing it on their lap.

Some small harps are designed to be worn with a shoulder strap (like a guitar strap) supporting the harp, and the harp hanging between the harpist's knees, as shown on the left. A lap bar can help support this type of harp, making it more stable.

MUSIC STAND

Place your music stand to the left of your harp, as close to the harp as possible, so you don't need to turn your head too much to view both the strings and the music.

HAND POSITION

The thumb is up higher than the fingers, with the top joint of the thumb inclined a bit towards them, not bent backwards. The hand is slightly cupped, forming a hollow in the palm. The first three fingers are curved in a relaxed manner and contact the strings about ¼" inch from the tip of the fingers. <u>The little finger is never used, since its reach is not as long as the ring finger.</u> The wrists are in a little towards the strings. The bottom of the hand is turned out a bit so that the hand is not totally parallel to the strings. The fingers should rest lightly on the strings, near the center of each string. Relax the shoulders.

Both elbows should be up, so that the forearms are horizontal to the floor; don't rest your elbows on your legs. When playing the middle or high strings, the right forearm (or wrist for the upper strings) may rest on the side of the soundbox, but should not lean heavily on it. Your arm should be free to move easily up and down the harp. The left arm does not contact the soundbox.

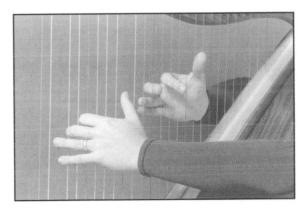

The photos on page 16 show the proper finger action:

Pluck the strings with the finger tips and bring the fingers into the palm of the hand. Use your whole finger in this action; don't just bend the first knuckle. Good sound is produced by using the whole finger and bringing it all the way into the palm. You don't need to worry about the little finger. It should naturally follow the ring finger into the palm.

Pluck the string with the side of the thumb and bring the thumb down until it touches the side of the first finger. Use your whole thumb in this action, not the top joint. Keep the top joint inclined forward a bit; don't let it bend backwards.

The fingernails should be short so they don't hamper the finger action. The nails should never touch the strings.

FUNDAMENTALS

We'll begin with some basic definitions:

MUSIC: a. beautiful, pleasing or interesting arrangements of sounds, especially as produced by the voice or instruments
b. written or printed signs for tones

TONE: a sound of definite pitch and duration

PITCH: the degree of highness or lowness of a sound or tone

DURATION: the time during which anything continues

NOTE: a. the written sign to show the pitch and length of a sound, e.g. ♩ ♪ ♩ 𝅝
b. same as tone

Written music is like a map or a diagram of the sounds we hear. The notes are symbols that tell us the pitch and duration of each sound.

Notes are named using the first seven letters of the alphabet: A, B, C, D, E, F, G.

On the harp, all C strings are colored red, and all F strings are blue or black or green. Find one red string on your harp. This is a C. The next higher string in pitch (going up toward the shorter strings on your harp) is a D. The next string is an E. The next is blue or black and is an F. After that is G, A, B and back again to another red C, and so on.

From one string to the next string of the <u>same letter name</u> (i.e. from C to C, or from G to G, etc) is called an <u>octave</u>.

Practice touching various strings on your harp and say their names out loud until you feel certain of them.

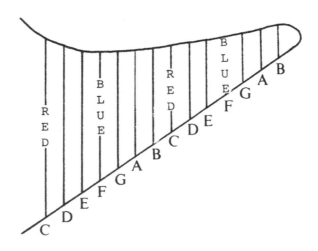

HOW TO READ MUSIC

Notes are written on a set of five lines called a <u>staff</u> or <u>stave</u>:
The placement of notes on the staff tells you the relative pitch
of the tones. In this example, the first note is lower in pitch
than the second note.

<u>Ledger lines</u> are added above or below the staff to increase the
range of the staff.

We do not know the exact pitch of the notes on the staff until we add a <u>clef</u>. A
clef is a symbol which is placed on a staff that indicates what tones the notes
represent.

This is a <u>treble clef</u>: . When it is placed on a staff, these are the names of
the notes on the staff.

To find middle C on your harp, locate the red string that has at least 14 strings
above it and at least 7 strings (preferably 10) below it. For the purposes of
this book, that is middle C.

One way to help you learn which note on the staff corresponds with which letter,
is to make words or phrases out of the letters of the lines and spaces of the
staff. For example:

LINES

Every Good Boy Does Fine
or   Every Good Bird Does Fly

SPACES

F - A - C - E

To help you learn the names of the notes on the staff, go through the pieces in
the first four lessons of this book and name each note. Do this until you feel
certain about the notes and their names.

Each piece of music has a definite beat or pulse. When you clap your hands to a piece, you are clapping to the beats.

Notes ♩ consist of a body ● and a stem │ . These are used to indicate the time value of a note, that is, how many beats it should be held, or its duration.

𝅝 = 4 beats   A <u>whole note</u> has an open body with no stem. It is held 4 beats.

𝅗𝅥 = 2 beats   A <u>half note</u> has an open body and a stem. It is held half as long as a whole note, or 2 beats.

♩ = 1 beat   A <u>quarter</u> note has a filled-in body and a stem. It is held one-quarter as long as a whole note, or 1 beat.

Notes can be written with their stems up or down, it doesn't matter. The pitch of the note is indicated by the position of the body of the note on the staff, not by the stem. For example, these notes are all B's.

Music is divided into units of time called <u>measures</u>. The dividing line between two measures is called a <u>bar line</u>. A <u>double bar</u> indicates the end of a piece or a section of a piece.

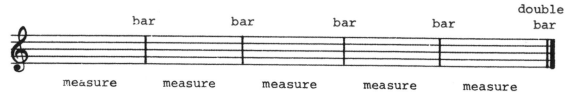

All of the measures in one piece will contain the same number of beats. A <u>time signature</u> (e.g. $\frac{3}{4}$ or $\frac{4}{4}$) will be written at the beginning of a piece to tell you how many beats there are in each measure.

$\frac{3}{4}$ time means that there will be the equivalent of 3 quarter notes, or 3 beats in each measure.

$\frac{4}{4}$ time means that there will be the equivalent of 4 quarter notes, or 4 beats in each measure.

14

When learning a new piece of music, you must be sure that you hold each note the proper number of beats. The best way to ensure this is to count each measure out loud as you play it.

If you are playing in $\frac{4}{4}$ time, you count "1 2 3 4 1 2 3 4 1 2 3 4" etc. evenly at the speed you want to play the piece.

In $\frac{3}{4}$ time, count "1 2 3 1 2 3 1 2 3" etc.

Here are some examples of measures in $\frac{4}{4}$ time and how to count them. In these examples, count "1 2 3 4" in each measure, but only play on the counts circled.

Count "1 2 3 4". Play on all 4 counts since each note gets 1 beat.

Count "1 2 3 4". Play only on beat 1 since a whole note is held four beats.

Count "1 2 3 4". Play on beat 1 and beat 3 since half notes get two beats each.

Count "1 2 3 4". Play on beat 1 and then on beats 3 and 4.

Count "1 2 3 4". Play on beats 1, 2 and 3.

Here are some examples of measures in $\frac{3}{4}$ time. Count "1 2 3" in each measure, but only play on the circled counts.

Count "1 2 3". Play on all three beats since each note gets one beat.

Count "1 2 3". Play on beats 1 and 3. The first note is held two beats.

Count "1 2 3". Play on beats 1 and 2. The second note is held two beats.

Lesson 1

In this book, the fingers of both hands will be numbered as follows:

Thumb	Index Finger	Middle Finger	Ring Finger
1	2	3	4

Since the little finger is never used, it is not numbered.

❖❖❖

Placing the fingers on the strings before they are needed is an important aspect of harp technique. It provides stability for your fingers and enables you to play more quickly.

A bracket ⌐ ⌐ or ⌐___⌐ is used to indicate fingers that should be placed together. The fingers should be placed on all the notes within the bracket before the first note in the bracket is played.

For example, when playing four ascending notes, such as ⌐C, D, E, F⌐ all four fingers should be placed on their respective strings before playing the first note. Then the strings are plucked one at a time by bringing the fingers into the palm. After all notes in the bracket have been played, the hand should be closed with all fingers in the palm and the thumb resting on top of the second finger.

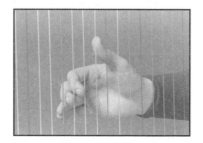 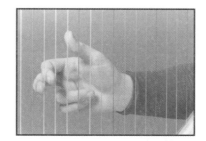 

 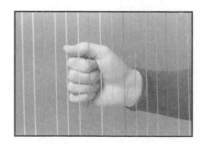

The beginning of Exercise 1 A is played as follows:
   a. place fingers 2 and 1 on the strings
   b. play finger 2
   c. play finger 1
   d. place fingers 2 and 1 on the next strings
   e. play finger 2
   f. play finger 1
   etc.

In Exercise 1 B, three fingers are placed at once; and in Exercise 1 C, all four
fingers are placed together.

Practice these exercises first with the right hand, and then with the left hand an
octave lower. Practice them slowly, being sure that all the fingers in the brackets
are placed before you begin.

EXERCISE 1 A

EXERCISE 1 B

EXERCISE 1 C

At the beginning of each piece in this book is a word indicating the speed at which it should be played. These are the terms I use, in order from the slowest to the fastest.

very slowly
slowly
leisurely
moderately
briskly
fast
very fast

Also, many pieces have a second word indicating a feeling or emotion (i.e. tenderly, happily, mournfully, etc.). All of these terms are meant only to give a general guideline for the piece.

❖❖

When placing the fingers in a bracket, place only the fingers indicated, or you will become confused. That is, if the bracket is ⌊ 4 2 1 ⌋ , don't place finger 3 on a string. Any finger that is not being used is held near the palm.

❖❖

Practice these pieces first with the right hand and then with the left an octave lower. Be sure to count the beats as you play.

Twinkle, Twinkle, Little Star

MODERATELY

Yankee Doodle

BRISKLY

❖❖

Go Tell Aunt Rhodie

MODERATELY

❖❖

An <u>eighth note</u> has a filled-in body, a stem, and a flag. This is an eighth note ♪
It is held 1/2 beat. Therefore, two eighth notes are equal to one quarter note.
Two or more eighth notes can be grouped together with a line (called a beam)
replacing the flags: ♪♪ = ♫   ♪♪♪♪ = ♫♫

When counting the beats in a measure that contains eighth notes, you still count
"1 2 3 4" as before, but you add the word "and" <u>between</u> each number to create 8
divisions like this: "1 and 2 and 3 and 4 and". Be sure that the basic 1-2-3-4
beat stays the same as it was before. One way to practice this is to clap your
hands in a steady beat and count one number on each clap; then, keeping your
claps steady, add the word "and" between each clap, like this:

```
clap      clap      clap      clap      clap      clap      clap      clap
1         2         3         4         1    and  2    and  3    and  4    and
```

Here are some examples using eighth notes. In these examples, count " 1 & 2 & 3 & 4 &" in each measure, but only play on the circled counts.

❖❖❖

These pieces have eighth notes in them. Count them very carefully. Practice first with your right hand and then with your left an octave lower.

Lavender's Blue

SLOWLY

❖❖❖

Are You Sleeping?

MODERATELY

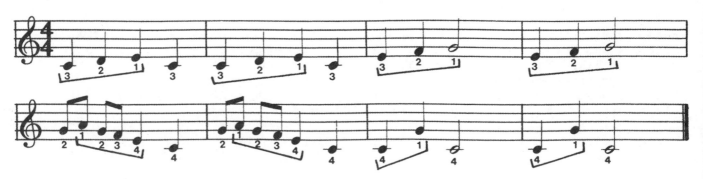

Lesson 2

This symbol ♩ is a <u>quarter rest</u>. It gets one beat of silence. When you get to this rest you count one beat, but don't play anything. For example, several measures in The Water is Wide (the next piece) have a rest on the first beat. You still count "1 2 3 4", but do not play anything on beat 1.

Sometimes brackets overlap each other, as in the following exercise. This exercise should be played as follows:

    a. Place all four fingers on the first four notes (C, D, E, F)

    b. Play the first three notes (C, D, E)

    c. Before playing the thumb (keeping it placed), place the 4th finger on the first note of the next measure (D)

    d. Play the thumb, keeping the 4th finger placed

    e. Place the other fingers (3, 2, 1) for the second measure

    f. Repeat from b.

Place 4, 3, 2, 1 | before playing 1, place 4 | place 3, 2, 1 | before playing 1 place 4   etc.

Play this exercise first with the right hand, and then with the left hand an octave lower.

EXERCISE 2

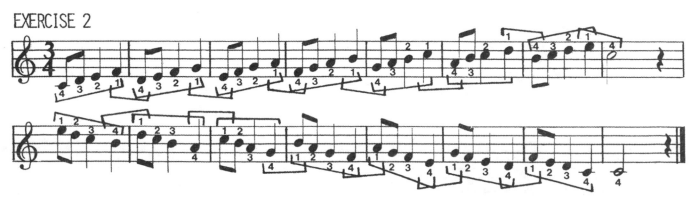

All of the pieces in this lesson should be played first with the right hand and then with the left hand an octave lower.

Remember to place all the fingers within the brackets, but only those that you need.

The Water is Wide

VERY SLOWLY

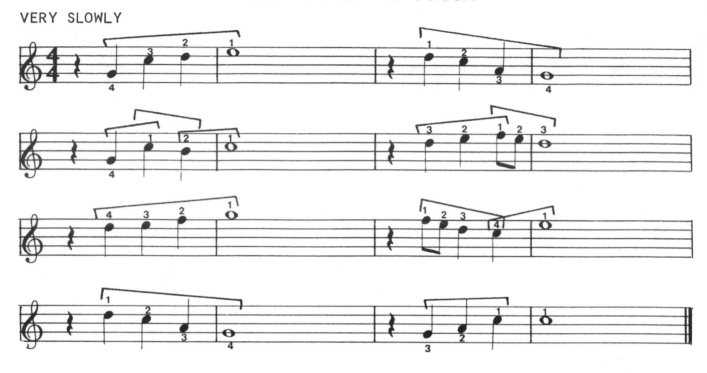

White Choral Bells

LEISURELY

Long, Long Ago

Two notes of the same pitch can be <u>tied</u> together like this: You pluck only the first note, but hold it for the combined duration of both notes. In this example you play the G only once, but hold it for 8 full beats. In this next piece, there are tied notes at the end of the 4th and 8th staves.

SLOWLY

A <u>dot</u> following a note increases the value of the note by <u>one-half of its original value.</u>

♩ = 2 beats   ♩. = 3 beats

♩ = 1 beat   ♩. = 1½ beats

Here are some examples of dotted notes and how to count them. You would play on the circled counts.

count ①2 3 ④ ①②3 4 ① & 2 &③& ④ & ① & 2 &③ & 4 & ① & 2 &③ & 4 &

Country Gardens

Country Gardens was originally a Morris dance tune. A Morris dance is an old English dance performed in costume or disguise. The dancers often wore bells on their legs.

MODERATELY

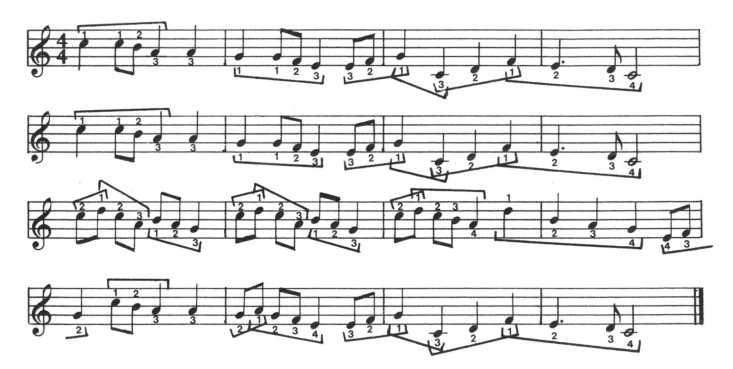

Allemande

An Allemande is a dance that was popular during the Renaissance.

BRISKLY & COURTLY

T. ARBEAU

~~~~~~~~~~~~~~~~~~~~~~~~~~~~~~

Lesson 3

Rests are symbols that indicate periods of silence. There are several kinds of rests, and each one gets a certain number of beats. Here are the rests and their time values.

4 beats	2 beats	1 beat	½ beat
whole rest	half rest	quarter rest	eighth rest

Rests can be dotted, just like notes. Therefore,

𝄾. = 1½ beats.

Throughout the rest of the book, two staves will be joined together. They are
played at the same time. Notes on the top staff are played with the right hand, RH
and notes on the bottom staff are played with the left hand. LH

In this exercise, the left hand plays an octave lower than the written music.
In the other pieces in this lesson, however, the left hand will play as written
(not an octave lower).

EXERCISE 3

Joy To The World

BRISKLY

GEORGE F. HANDEL

Blue Bells of Scotland

The first note of this song is in a measure all by itself, even though it only
gets one beat. This is called a "pick-up". When this occurs, the last measure
of the song will also have fewer beats than normal. The pick-up plus the last
measure will always equal one full measure.

MODERATELY & MARCHLIKE

Minuet

BRISKLY, WITH RESTRAINT

J. S. BACH

Lesson 4

In this lesson you will begin to play with both hands at the same time. Before you start this lesson, go back and play everything in the first three lessons with <u>both hands at the same time</u>. Play the left hand an octave lower than the right. This will help you get used to both hands playing together.

These are <u>repeat signs</u> 𝄆 𝄇. They indicate that when you get to the second sign, go back to the first sign, repeat that section, then continue. For example:

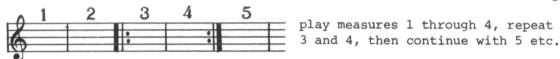

play measures 1 through 4, repeat 3 and 4, then continue with 5 etc.

If there is only the second sign, then repeat from the beginning. For example:

play measures 1 through 4, repeat 1 through 4, continue with 5 etc.

EXERCISE 4

This exercise is to get your fingers accustomed to one hand going up while the other goes down. Both hands play at the same time. Repeat it through several times until it flows well. Don't worry if at first your fingers get confused and go the wrong way. This exercise is a bit like trying to pat your head and rub your stomach at the same time. Keep practicing; you'll get it.

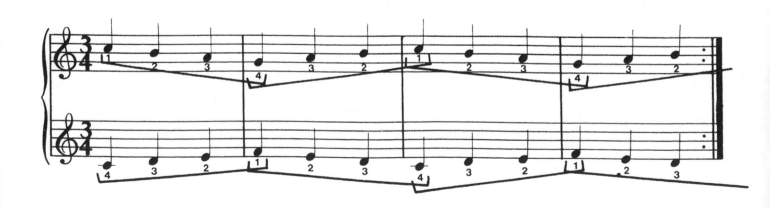

Throughout the rest of this book, practice the right and and the left hand
separately a few times and then learn the piece with both hands together.

~~~~~~~~~~~~~~~~~~~~~~~~~~~~~~~~~~

All Through the Night

Remember to repeat :‖ the first line of this piece.

VERY SLOWLY, A LULLABY   WALES

In this book I use parentheses (♩) to indicate notes that are part of the melody, or main tune, but that are played by the left hand rather than the right. I write the note in both clefs so you can see the continuity of the melody; but the note in parentheses is not played, as it is duplicated in the left hand.

Robin Adair

LEISURELY & SIMPLY

SCOTLAND/IRELAND

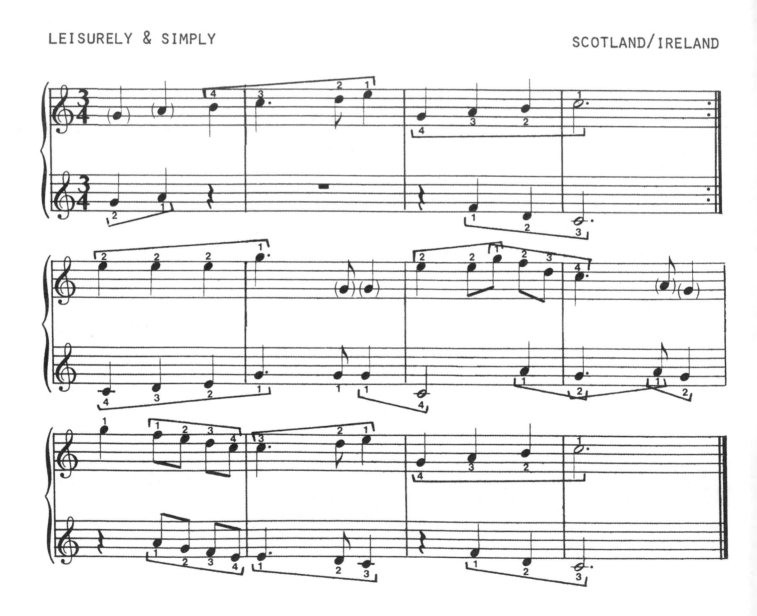

Ode to Joy

MODERATELY & MAJESTICALLY

BEETHOVEN

Lesson 5

Most harp music (as well as piano and organ music) is written in two clefs: the treble clef , which we have already learned, and the bass clef  . Usually, the right hand will play what is written in the treble clef, and the left hand will play what is written in the bass clef. Here are the notes that you will need to know in the bass clef:

Notice that middle C can be written in either clef:    or   These are both the same string.

These other notes can also be written in either clef:

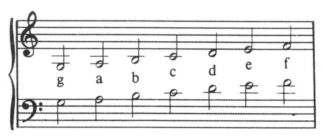

If your harp only has 7 strings below middle C, you will not be able to play the three lowest notes that are used in this book. When these are written in the music, play them an octave higher, as shown here.

To help you learn the bass clef, phrases can be made out of the letters of the notes of the lines and spaces, as we did for the treble clef. For example:

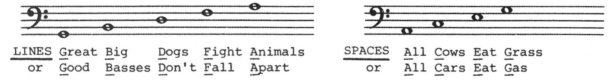

LINES	Great	Big	Dogs	Fight	Animals
or	Good	Basses	Don't	Fall	Apart

SPACES	All	Cows	Eat	Grass
or	All	Cars	Eat	Gas

Go through some of the pieces in the rest of the book and name the notes in the bass clef. Do this until you feel certain about their names.

In this exercise, place your fingers on the strings one measure ahead. For example, while playing the left hand, place the right hand on the notes in the next measure. Then, while playing your right, place your left, etc. In this manner, try to play the exercise without having to stop at the end of each measure to place.

EXERCISE 5

Drink to Me Only with Thine Eyes

The origin of this tune is unknown, but it is commonly used with the poem by Ben Jonson, written in 1616.

SLOWLY   ENGLAND

Planxty George Brabazon

Turlough O'Carolan (1670-1738) is the best known of the Irish harpers. About 200
of his tunes are extant, and many more tunes are falsely attributed to him. He
began studying the harp at the age of 18 when he was blinded by smallpox. At 21
he set out with a horse, a guide, and his harp to make his way as an itinerant
harper. He was welcomed into the best houses in Ireland and was always treated
with respect and esteem. Many of his pieces are "planxties", or songs written
in honor of his patrons or members of their households. He sometimes used well-
known tunes and wrote new words for them. Only a few of his lyrics still exist.
This planxty was written in honor of George Brabazon of County Mayo, who was then
a young bachelor. The tune is known in Scotland as Twa Bonnie Maidens.

BRISKLY & BOLDLY   CAROLAN

Scarborough Fair

LEISURELY, WITH A LILT

Before you begin this lesson, go back and re-read the pages about how to hold
the harp and hand position to be sure that you are playing correctly

Lesson 6

EXERCISE 6 A

EXERCISE 6 B

EXERCISE 6 C

The Grenadier and the Lady

LEISURELY & FIRMLY

ENGLAND

As you already know, a quarter note ♩ gets one beat, or two eighth notes ♫ get one beat. Sometimes three notes get one beat. This is called a triplet All three notes are of equal value (1/3 of a beat) and in total they get one beat. There is a triplet in the fourth measure of this next piece. To count this triplet measure, say "1 & 2 & 3 & 4 & uh". The "4 & uh" are the 3 notes of the triplet and are said and played a little faster than the other counts.

My Love is Like A Red, Red Rose

At the end of this piece are the Italian words DC al Fine. DC stands for "da capo"
or "from the beginning" and "al Fine" means "to the end". It means that when you
get to the "DC al Fine" you go back to the beginning and play through to where it
says "Fine" or "end". In this piece you play to the end of the written music,
start over and play through to the double bar in the 8th measure.

This is the tune that is commonly used with Robert Burns' poem of this name.

SLOWLY & TENDERLY   SCOTLAND

Searching for Lambs

This piece is in $\frac{5}{4}$ time, which means that there are 5 beats in each measure. Don't be surprised if this seems unnatural to you. It is a rare time signature for Western music. Count it very carefully as you learn it to be sure you have it right.

Also notice that the left hand changes from the bass clef to the treble clef, and then back again to the bass clef. This is done to reduce the number of ledger lines.

MODERATELY & HAUNTINGLY   BRITISH ISLES

❖❖

Both of the next two pieces are in $\frac{6}{8}$ time. That means that there are 6 beats in each measure, but that an <u>eighth</u> note (rather than a quarter note) gets one beat. Therefore, these are the time values of the notes in these pieces:

♪ = 1 beat (eighth note)

♪. = 1½ beat (dotted eighth note)

♩ = 2 beats (quarter note)

♩. = 3 beats (dotted quarter note)

There is another kind of note in these pieces: the <u>sixteenth note</u> ♬. It has two flags. It is held half as long as an eighth note, or ½ beat. Two or more sixteenth notes can be written together with two beams replacing the two flags: ♫ = ♪♪

When sixteenth notes are written with dotted
eighth notes, only part of the beam is
written next to the sixteenth note:

In these pieces, sixteenth notes are written
in one of the two following ways. The two
ways are written a bit differently, but they
mean the same thing.

count ① & 2 &③ & or ① & 2 &③ &

Greensleeves   or   What Child is This?

LEISURELY & ROMANTICALLY

ENGLAND

Planxty Irwin

The repeat signs ‖: :‖ in this piece indicate that you play section A twice and then play section B twice.

Carolan wrote this planxty for Colonel John Irwin of County Sligo, Ireland.

LEISURELY & FLOWINGLY

CAROLAN

Lesson 7

EXERCISE 7

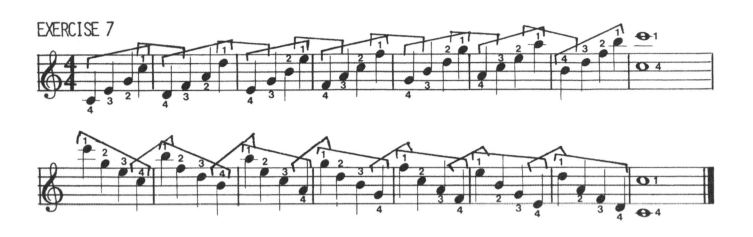

Sometimes when a section of a piece is repeated, the last measure (or several measures) is different the second time through. This ⌐1.⌐ is placed over the ending measure that is played the first time through, and this ⌐2.⌐ is placed over the measure that is played instead the second time. For example:

play measures 1 through 5, go back to the beginning and play 1 through 4, SKIP 5, and play 6 instead, continue with 7 etc.

1   2   3   4   5   6   7

This occurs twice in the next piece as follows:
 a. play the first half of the piece with the first ending
 b. repeat the first half of the piece with the second ending instead
 c. continue with the second half of the piece using the new first ending
 d. repeat the second half of the piece using the new second ending.

Trip To Sligo   or   Lark on the Strand

LEISURELY & HAPPILY

IRELAND

46

Minuet

MODERATELY

J. S. BACH

Farewell

SLOWLY & EMOTIONALLY   HIGHLANDS OF SCOTLAND

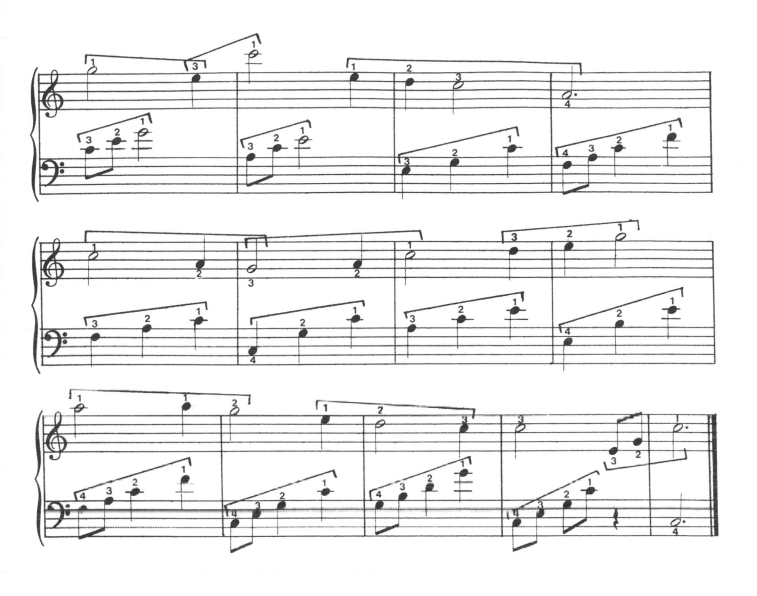

Lesson 8

A chord is two or more notes that are played at the same time. In this lesson, two-note chords are played with one hand.

This exercise is played with one hand. Practice with the right hand and then with the left an octave lower. Then play both hands together.

EXERCISE 8

The Christ Child's Lullaby

SLOWLY & TENDERLY

HEBRIDES

Cherry Blooms

LEISURELY

JAPAN

St. Anthony's Chorale

MODERATELY & STATELY

JOSEPH HAYDN

Lesson 9

Chords of three or more notes are usually "broken". This means that rather than play all the notes together at the same time, you "break" the chord, playing the notes in rapid succession from the lowest note to the highest note. Do this very quickly. This is what gives the chords their characteristic "harp-like" sound. Chords are always broken from the bottom to the top, that is, from the lowest note to the highest.

EXERCISE 9 A

EXERCISE 9 B

EXERCISE 9 C

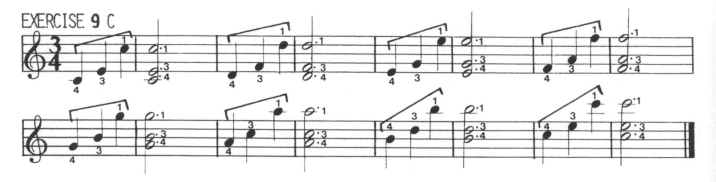

This sign 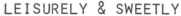 is a <u>fermata</u>, meaning "pause" in German or Italian. This means to hold the note a bit longer than usual (or pause on it) before continuing. If you are counting the beats in the measure, stop counting at the fermata and pause before continuing to count.

Lullaby

In this piece, the melody begins in the left hand and then continues with the right. Also, notice that both hands are written in the treble clef.

LEISURELY & SWEETLY   WALES

Johnny has Gone for a Soldier

In this piece the melody, or tune, is played with the left hand.

SLOWLY & MOURNFULLY

USA

Flow Gently, Sweet Afton

The words to "Flow Gently Sweet Afton" were written by Robert Burns. This tune
can also be used with "Away in a Manger".

LEISURELY & PEACEFULLY   ALEXANDER HUME — SCOTLAND

theme from the
New World Symphony

SLOWLY & STATELY

ANTON DVORAK

Lesson 10

EXERCISE 10 A

EXERCISE 10 B

EXERCISE 10 C

EXERCISE 10 D

Cockles and Mussels

LEISURELY & SIMPLY

Au Clair de la Lune

This song, written by the opera composer in the court of Louis XIV, became a popular folk song in France.

MODERATELY & SIMPLY

J. B. LULLY

Shenandoah

VERY SLOWLY & FLOWING

USA

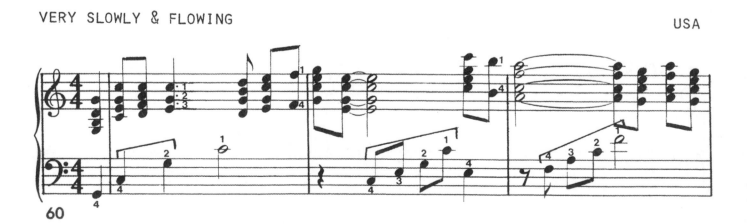

60

Lesson 11

When playing 5 consecutive descending notes, it is often best to <u>slide</u> the thumb from the first to the second note. This ⌐1 1⌐ indicates that the thumb should slide. For example, in the first measure of this exercise, place your fingers on G, E, D, C (skipping the F string). Slide your thumb across the G and F and then play the E, D, C as usual. Be sure to slide rather than pluck with your thumb. Practice this exercise until all 5 notes in each group sound even.

EXERCISE 11 A

"Cross-overs" and "cross-unders" are techniques used when playing a series of 5 or more notes that are either all ascending or all descending. These techniques are slight variations on the methods of placing discussed in the first two lessons.

Example 1: Ascending (cross-unders)

    a. place all 4 fingers on the first 4 strings (C, D, E, F)
    b. play fingers 4, 3, and 2
    c. before playing 1, bring 4 under the thumb and place it on G
    d. play the thumb
    e. pivot the hand towards you on the 4th finger so that the hand and fingers
       are in the proper position
    f. place 3, 2, and 1
    g. play 4, 3, 2, and 1

This can also be done by crossing the 3rd finger under, instead of the 4th, as in Exercise 11 C.

Example 2: Descending (cross-overs)

    a. place all 4 fingers on the first 4 strings (C, B, A, G)
    b. play fingers 1, 2, and 3
    c. before playing 4, bring the thumb over 4 and place it on the F
    d. play 4
    e. open the hand down from the thumb so that the fingers are in the proper
       position
    f. place 2, 3, and 4
    g. play 1, 2, 3, and 4

This can also be done using only three fingers (1, 2, and 3) with the thumb crossing over the 3rd finger, as in Exercise 11 C.

EXERCISE 11 B

EXERCISE 11 C

Gilliekrankie

This tune was probably written by a 17th Century Irish harper named Thomas Connelan who was living in Scotland. It commemorates a battle fought in Scotland in 1689.

BRISKLY & MARCH-LIKE

SCOTLAND

In these exercises, the cross-overs or cross-unders are followed by chords. The sequence is the same as in the examples before Exercise 11B, except that one finger is left out in steps f and g (i.e. the chords in Exercise D don't use the 3rd finger, and the chords in Exercise E don't use the 2nd finger).

EXERCISE 11 D

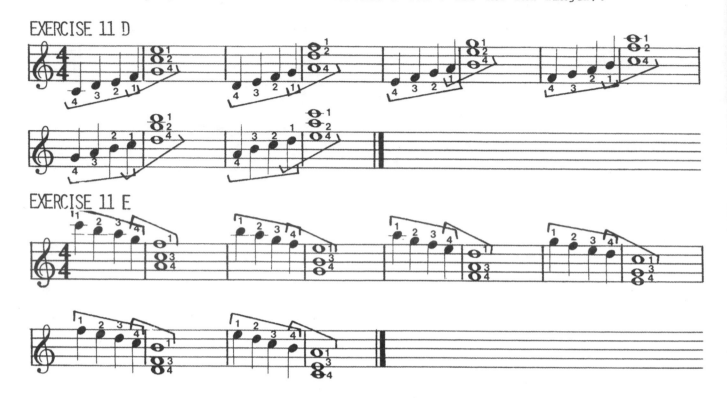

EXERCISE 11 E

When a bracket contains one or more notes followed by a chord, only one finger for the chord is placed at the beginning of the bracket. In these examples, finger 1 from the chord is placed with the finger(s) for the first note(s). The other fingers in the chord are placed right before the chord is played.

Ash Grove

LEISURELY & EMOTIONALLY   WALES

Wild Mountain Thyme

Robert Tannahill (1774-1810)., a weaver in Paisley, Scotland, wrote words to this tune.
SLOWLY & LONGINGLY

Lesson 12

A glissando, commonly called a "gliss"  or  is the best known and most easily recognizable harp effect. It is produced by sliding a finger either up or down along the strings. A gliss can be played slowly or quickly and can cover a few or many notes. Often ascending and descending glisses are played alternately, producing a wave-like effect. Ascending glisses are played with the fleshy part of finger 2. Descending ones are played with the thumb.

This ascending gliss begins on the lower C at the beginning of beat 1, and ends on the higher C at the beginning of beat 2. The length of the gliss is always the number of beats of the first note (i.e. this first note gets one beat, so the gliss itself gets that one beat).

Practice playing ascending and descending glisses with both hands (separately) at various speeds until all of the notes sound even.

❖❖❖

A harmonic is a method of playing a string so that it sounds an octave higher than its normal pitch. This is done by touching the string in the center so that only half of the string vibrates, and then plucking the string. The note produced has a lovely bell-like sound.

Harmonics are played differently with the right and left hands.

RIGHT HAND
Curl the fingers in towards the palm. Press the first knuckle of finger 2 against the center of the string. Keep the thumb up. Gently pluck the string with the thumb and move the hand away from the string at the same time. Don't force it.

LEFT HAND
Place the fleshy part of the side of the hand (below the little finger) against the middle of the string. The thumb should be up with the fingers relaxed, not in to the palm. Pluck the string gently with the thumb and move the hand away from the string at the same time. Don't force it.

RIGHT
HAND

LEFT (seen from the
HAND   right hand side
       of the harp)

Harmonics are clear only at the center of the strings. Move your hand up and down near the center of the string until you find the spot where the harmonic is the clearest. Be sure to keep your thumb high to get the best possible harmonic.

Harmonics are written where they are played, and sound an octave higher. In other words, when reading music, play the harmonic on the string that is written, but it will produce a sound an octave higher.

Harmonics are written like this:

Practice harmonics with both hands until they are clear.

❖❖

Minstrel Boy

MODERATELY & MARCH-LIKE   IRELAND

Southwind

SLOWLY & BEAUTIFULLY   IRELAND

Sheebeg Sheemore

Carolan used this melody (originally called The Bonny Cuckoo) and wrote words to it for his first composition. The lyrics told about a battle between the fairies of Sheebeg (the Little Fairy Hill) and Sheemore (the Big Fairy Hill).

LEISURELY & LILTINGLY

Jesu, Joy of Man's Desiring

MODERATELY & EXPRESSIVELY

J. S. BACH

CONGRATULATIONS! You have now completed this book. You're a real harper! Write and let me know how it went, and I'll send you information on the next book in this series.

APPENDIX
TUNING YOUR HARP

Learning to tune your harp is an important part of learning to play, and it is essential that you keep your harp in tune by tuning it daily. New harps go out of tune quickly, because all of the strings are new and still stretching. Changes in temperature and humidity will also cause the strings to go out of tune. So, you should tune your harp every day before you sit down to play.

You should have received a tuning key, also called a tuning wrench, with your harp. Here's a photo of a variety of keys used by different harpmakers. Be sure to use the correct size key that fits your harp's tuning pins.

You can tune your harp to the notes on a piano or a pitch pipe. However, the easiest way to tune is with the help of a chromatic electronic tuner, which you can purchase from a harp store or other music store. When using an electronic tuner, you don't have to have a good "ear"; the tuner will tell you when a string is at the correct pitch. Follow the instructions that come with your electronic tuner. If you need more help, you'll find some tuner demonstrations at www.harpcenter.com.

Don't be surprised if you get frustrated when you're first learning to tune. It takes time to get a feel for which tuning pin is which, and how far you need to turn the tuning key. But, fortunately, the more you tune your harp, the faster you'll get! Just like learning to play your harp, learning to tune takes practice. Every time you tune you'll be a little bit quicker and more efficient, and soon you'll be tuning like a pro!

TUNING BASICS
Hold your tuning key in your right hand, and place it on the square end of the tuning pin for the string you are going to tune. Be sure the tuning key is on the correct pin, or you will tend to break strings by tightening them too much.

Pluck the string with your left hand. While it is still sounding, turn the tuning key until the electronic tuner indicates that the string is in tune. Or, if you are tuning to a piano, turn the tuning key until the pitch of the string matches the same pitch on the piano.

Some harps have zither pins, which are tuning pins that do not go through both sides of the neck of the harp, but are screwed into the neck on the side where the strings are attached. If your harp has zither pins, you might find it easiest to tune with the harp turned around backwards, with the front pillar towards you. Then you can hold the tuning key in your right hand and pluck the string with your left hand, as you would with harps with other types of tuning pins.

TUNING A NEW HARP
When tuning a new harp, or one that is not tuned up to pitch, always tune the lowest string first and then tune the strings consecutively all the way to the top. This allows the soundboard to adjust to the tension of the strings. After you have tuned all of the strings, start again at the bottom and repeat the whole process. This will need to be done quite a few times on a new harp before the strings stretch and adjust to their pitches.

SHARPS, FLATS, AND KEY SIGNATURES

Although there are no sharps (♯) or flats (♭) in any of the pieces in this book, you need to know what they are, and how to play them on your harp.

Most harps are equipped with sharping levers right below the bridge pins. When a lever is engaged (usually by flipping it up), it shortens the sounding length of the string, thereby raising the pitch by one half-step (also called a semitone).

In music, a sharp sign (♯) raises the pitch of a note by a half-step, such as from a white key on the piano up to the adjacent higher black key. For example, pluck an F string on your harp. This is called an F-natural (F♮). Now engage the sharping lever on that string, and pluck it again. You'll hear that the note is now higher in pitch. The sharping lever has shortened the sounding length of the string and raised the pitch by a half-step, making an F-sharp (F♯). A flat sign (♭) lowers the pitch of a note by a half-step, such as from a white key on the piano down to the adjacent lower black key. In written music, the sharp or natural signs are written in front of the note, as shown here on the right.

A key signature is the group of sharps or flats written at the beginning of a piece after the clef sign, and before the time signature. The key signature tells you what notes will be sharp or flat throughout the piece. In the example on the left, you would engage all of your F and C levers (making F♯s and C♯s) before you begin to play. You haven't noticed key signatures in the music in this book because the pieces have no sharps or flats, and therefore, the key signature area is left blank. (You can find more information on keys and key signatures in my Music Theory and Arranging Techniques for Folk Harps book.)

HARP TUNING METHODS

If your harp has a full set of sharping levers, you have a variety of ways you can tune your harp.

If all of your sharping levers are down (disengaged) and you tune every string to natural, like the white notes on the piano, you are tuned to the key of C. If you pluck a C string and play a scale up to the next C, you should hear a do-re-mi scale. When your harp is tuned like this, you can use your sharping levers and play pieces that have sharps in the key signature or within the piece.

However, if you want to play pieces that have flats in them, you need to tune some of your strings to flats. Start with all of your sharping levers down (disengaged). Then lower the pitch of the strings you want flat by one half-step by loosening the string with your tuning key. For example, tune all of your B strings to B♭ (on many electronic tuners, this will register as A♯). Then, when you use a sharping lever on a B string, the lever will raise the pitch up to a B♮. The most common flat tuning is to tune to 3 flats (also called the key of E♭) by tuning all of your B, E, and A strings to flats: (B♭, E♭ and A♭). In this tuning, with a full set of sharping levers, you can play in any key from 3 flats up to 4 sharps. For more information on tuning, see the tuning video at www.harpcenter.com/stringing.

If your harp has no sharping levers, you will need to re-tune your harp every time you change key signatures.

ACCIDENTALS AND LEVER CHANGES

An accidental is a sharp, flat, or natural within the piece that is not in the key signature. When this occurs you usually will need to either engage or disengage the sharping lever on that string. There are no accidentals or lever changes in this book, but you will find them in other harp books.

Because F♯ is not in the key signature in the example on the right, the F♯ in the second measure is an accidental. You will need to engage the sharping lever on this F string sometime after you play the F♮ in the first measure and before you play the F♯. Because you will move the lever with your left hand, you need to have a beat or two free in the bass clef to give you enough time to flip the lever. Sometimes the easiest time to flip the lever may be several measures before it is needed in the music.

There are several ways that lever changes are notated in harp music. All of the examples below on the left tell you to engage the lever on the F string above middle C during the second measure, after you play the low E with your left hand on beat 1, and before you play the F♯ with your right hand.

The "High" and "Low" Octave Method

This is the method that I use in most of my books. "Middle" or "mid" means the notes from middle C up to the next B, and "high" is the next higher octave, etc, as shown on the right.

The Pedal Harp Octave Method

This method numbers the octaves the way they do on pedal harps. The octaves go from an F on the bottom up to an E on top, as shown here.

The Diamond Note Method

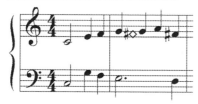

A diamond note is placed on the staff indicating which lever needs to be moved. You do NOT play the diamond note.

Before you play a piece, be sure to set your sharping levers to match the key signature, and follow any other lever instructions written at the beginning of the piece. Sometimes a lever chart will be printed at the top of the page, particularly if the lever settings are unusual.

Harp music will often indicate pedal changes for pedal harpists as well as the lever changes for lever harp players. When this happens, pedal changes are generally written below the bass staff, while lever changes are written between the treble and bass staves.

TAKING CARE OF YOUR HARP

If you take proper care of your harp, it should give you decades of pleasure.

First, you need to decide where to keep the harp in your house. Never put your harp near a window where it will receive direct sunlight, and try to keep it away from heating and air conditioning vents. The more stable the environment (temperature and humidity), the happier your harp will be. An inside wall of the house is best, because the temperature tends to be more constant there than against an outside wall. Animals and small children (and even adults!) can easily knock over your harp if it is in an area with a lot of traffic. Whenever you finish playing, place your harp with its back resting lightly against your harp bench or chair, or the wall. That way, your harp is less likely to fall over.

Never leave your harp in a parked car, even for a short period of time. On a hot day the heat that builds up in a parked car can literally melt the glue that holds your harp together. Even if this damage may not be immediately evident to you, it can cause major problems for your harp at a later time. Cold can be just as bad for your harp. Freezing temperatures can crack some types of harp finish. So, to be safe, never leave your harp in a parked car!

Harps are happiest in an environment of about 40 - 50% relative humidity. If you live in a location where the humidity is very low, check with your harpmaker for recommendations to keep your harp safe.

Always wash your hands before you sit down to play your harp. Remove any jewelry that might scratch the harp. This can include watches, bracelets, necklaces, pins, and dangling earrings. Rhinestones and sequins on your blouse or t-shirt can also cause scratches. We've even seen harps that were damaged by belt buckles from people standing close to their harp while tuning. So, be careful when wearing anything that has any potential of damaging your beautiful instrument. When in doubt, take it off and keep it away from your harp.

Always cover your harp, or put it in its case, before putting it on a dolly or into your car. Be careful when moving your harp: it is easy to bash it into doorways and other obstacles if you are not paying close attention. Never leave your harp unattended while it is on a dolly or cart.

Keep your harp clean and dust-free with a plain, soft dust cloth. Never use any type of polish or wax on your harp unless it is recommended by your harpmaker. Harpmakers use a variety of lacquers and other finishes on their instruments. You do not want to put anything on your harp that will damage the finish, or make your harp greasy, or gummy. You can use a soft, clean paint brush or dust brush to clean the "hard-to-reach-places" around the pins, levers, and disks.

Always keep your harp tuned, and replace broken strings promptly with the correct type and gauge of string. Never tune your harp to a higher pitch than recommended by the harpmaker.

REPLACING STRINGS

It is not unusual for harp strings to break, so you need to learn to replace broken strings. Harpmakers use a variety of types and gauges of strings, and it is extremely important that you use the correct strings for your harp. You should have received a string chart or string list with your harp, showing the correct strings for your harp model. If not, contact your harpmaker or a harp store that specializes in strings, and get a correct string gauge chart for your harp model. It is a good idea to keep an extra set of strings with your harp, so you can replace the strings when they break. BE SURE TO REPLACE A BROKEN STRING WITH THE CORRECT GAUGE AND TYPE OF STRING.

STEP 1 - Remove the old string from the back of the soundbox, and from around the tuning pin. If the string is wire or metal, use pliers to remove the string, so you don't cut your fingers.

STEP 2 - Prepare the tuning pin. The next step depends on which of three types of tuning pins are on your harp. Most harps have **tapered pins**, which are fatter on the end where you put your tuning key, and taper down to a smaller diameter on the end where the string attaches. Before you put on your new string, make sure the tapered pin is securely seated in its hole. Use your tuning key to twist back and forth slightly as you push firmly in toward the neck of the harp.

Dusty Strings has been using **threaded tuning pins** on their harps since 1998. On the outside, they look similar to tapered pins, but they have threads in the middle, inside the neck of the harp. Both the tapered pins and the Dusty Strings threaded pins are types of "through pins," because the pins go all the way through the neck. Some harps by other makers have **zither pins**, which don't go all the way through the neck of the harp: they only stick out on one side of the neck.

If your harp has either Dusty Strings **threaded pins** or **zither pins**, use your tuning key to unscrew the pin 3 or 4 turns before attaching the new string. If you skip this step, the pin will be too far into the neck once you bring the new string up to pitch.

STEP 3 - Knot and insert the string. Wound strings and bass wire strings come with an anchor on one end. When replacing any other type of string, you will need to tie a knot in one end. See page 78 for instructions on how to tie this knot. Once you've tied the knot (or if the string has an anchor), insert the free end of the string from the inside of the soundbox up through the hole in the soundboard. Pull the string through until stopped by the knot or the anchor.

Another option is to thread the string through the hole BEFORE you tie the knot. To do this, insert the string through the hole from the TOP of the soundboard and then pull it through partway out the back of the soundbox and tie the knot. Pull the other end of the string back up through the soundboard until stopped by the knot.

STEP 4 - Thread the string through the tuning pin hole. Draw the string up to the tuning pin passing it through the sharping lever, if necessary, thread it through the hole in the tuning pin, and pull it taut. Be sure that the string is on the correct side of the bridge pin.

STEP 5 - Create slack in the string if necessary. Depending on what type of string you are replacing, you may need to leave some slack before you start to wind the string. You want to end up with the string wrapping about 3 or 4 times around the tuning pin once the string is staying up to pitch. If you have either too few or too many wraps, your string is much more likely to break.

The highest thin nylon or gut strings need the most slack of about 2", with the slack decreasing as the strings get thicker. Bass wires and other strings with a wire core need up to 2" to 3" of slack. You do not need to leave any slack for nylon or gut strings over a gauge of about .036 or in the 4th and 5th octaves, or for nylon wrapped strings with a nylon core. To create slack, pull the string to the side about 3 string spaces, or pull the string back down through the hole in the tuning pin the proper number of inches.

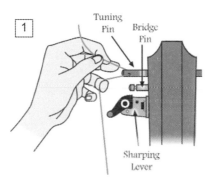

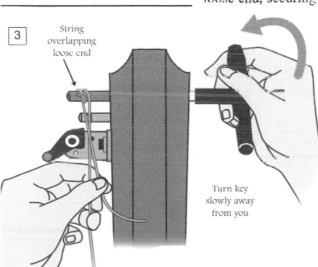

STEP 6 - Use your tuning key to wind the string on the tuning pin.
Hold the loose end of string out with your left hand as shown in Fig. 1. With your right hand, place your tuning key on the correct tuning pin and turn it by pushing your thumb away from you, until the string crosses over itself as shown in Fig. 2.

Bring this twist back toward the harp and continue turning the pin, so that the string winds over the loose end, securing it (Fig. 3).

Wind until the string has some tension and check to make sure the string is on the correct side of the bridge pin and tucked into the groove as shown in Fig. 4. Be sure the string looks like all of the other strings around it. Continue to slowly turn the pin with your tuning key until the string is up to the proper pitch. (If your harp has tapered pins, be sure to push the tuning key in towards the neck of the harp as you turn, to keep the tuning pin tight.)

STEP 7 - Cut off the excess string.
New strings, particularly nylon strings, need a lot of tuning before they will stay up to pitch. Once you're sure that the string is on your harp correctly, you should cut off the excess string above the tuning pin. On the highest strings, the excess will often be long enough to use later as another replacement string.

BASS WIRE STRINGS
Because harpmakers use a variety of types of wound bass wire strings, the instructions for replacing these strings varies greatly. Bass wire strings are particularly tricky to replace, and should be brought up to pitch slowly. Be very careful when replacing these strings, because if you make a mistake you usually will not be able to unwind the string and start over. Check with your harpmaker, your maker's website, or www.harpcenter.com to find additional instructions for the type of bass strings on your harp.

TYING THE HARP STRING KNOT

When replacing a gut or monofilament nylon string you need to tie a knot in one end, to secure the string against the soundboard. Here are two different ways to tie the knot; you can use either method you like. To reinforce the knot in the thin, high strings, you will need a short piece of a thick string, about 1" in length, which is called a toggle or a spline. This toggle is the dark piece in these illustrations. You can see videos and more information about knots and replacing strings at www.harpcenter.com/stringing.

THE TRADITIONAL HARP KNOT

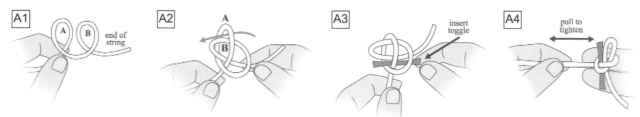

A1. Make two loops (A and B) near the end of the string.
A2. Insert loop B through loop A from back to front.
A3. For extra strength, and to be sure the knot won't pull up through the hole in the soundboard, insert a toggle through loop A.
A4. Pull loop A tight around loop B.

ALTERNATIVE HARP KNOT

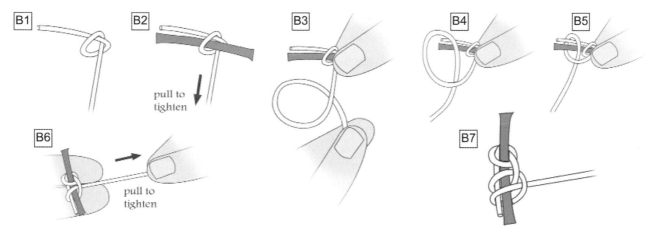

B1. Tie a loose standard knot, leaving about ½" to ¾" of string sticking out beyond the knot.
B2. Slide the toggle into the knot, lining it up parallel with the string end. Pull the long end of the string to tighten it around the toggle.
B3. Hold the knot and toggle with one hand and make a loop below the knot.
B4 and B5. Bring the loop up and tuck the string end and toggle through the loop.
B6. Pull the string to tighten.
B7. For higher (thinner) strings, repeat steps B3 through B6 to add a second loop knot. You'll end up with something that looks like figure B7: a knot that won't slip!

TABLE OF SYMBOLS

ALPHABETICAL INDEX OF TUNES

WHAT'S NEXT?

Once you have learned the pieces in this book, you have the basic skills you need to play the harp. I have written more than 20 books of music arranged specifically for folk harp, and there are hundreds more by other harpists and arrangers. You might want to wait a while before trying any books described as "advanced," but other than that, you should be able to choose any type of music you'd like: traditional, classical, religious, original, or popular music. You will need to learn to use your sharping levers, because many pieces have lever changes within the music. See pages 73 and 74 for more information.

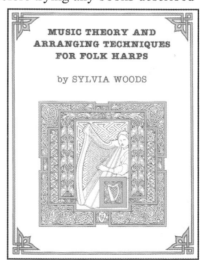

MUSIC THEORY AND ARRANGING TECHNIQUES FOR FOLK HARPS

by SYLVIA WOODS

My Music Theory and Arranging Techniques for Folk Harps book is the next book in this series. It teaches you the basic music theory and techniques you need to make your own arrangements. Subjects include chords, keys, inversions, transposing, accompaniment patterns, and much more. You can purchase this book from the store where you bought this book. Or, order it directly from www.harpcenter.com.